To _____Jennifer_____

With love from

_____Mom_____

A 3-minute forever book

EAT YOUR PEAS®

for New Moms

By Cheryl Karpen

Illustrated by Sandy Fougner

Congratulations!

Life
as you know it
is about to change forever.

And for the better!

Will it be easy?
Not on your life.

But it will be
wonderful.
Exhilarating. Exhausting.
Sometimes scary.
And always
surprising.

Which brings me to the reason
for this little book.

With all this **newness** in your life,
you are not alone.
I promise.

Want to talk?
Here's my number
(in case fatigue affects your memory)

919-469-0904   919-801-3415

Call me!

If you ever want to
brag a little
(or a lot),
if you ever need a good laugh,
a good cry,
or just some good old adult
conversation

Call me.

I promise to listen
(really listen)
with all my heart.

What's more, I promise I won't get
carried away with free advice
(unless, of course, you really,
really want some!)

In the meantime,
here's a little homegrown wisdom
to go with the wonder of your

new little sweet pea ...

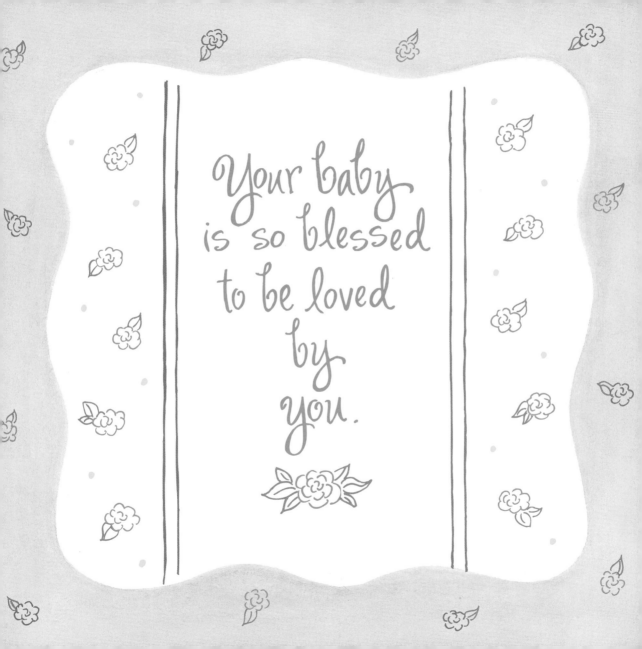

Your baby
is so blessed
to be loved
by
you.

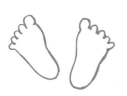

Get ready to experience
absolute
bliss
over a lot of
firsts!

first smile

first word

first burp

first coo

first step

May your days
be filled with
hugs and
giggles
and
silly things

only a mother could love.

When the baby keeps you
awake all night,
remember you will have
a lifetime to catch
up on your sleep.

But you'll never
have this night
with your little one again.

Trust
your instincts.

You
will be an
unbelievable
Mom.

There is nothing quite as sweet as baby toes.

Kiss them often!

What you didn't get right today you can practice again tomorrow.

(After all, isn't that what you will teach your Little One?)

Keep a **calendar** handy to jot down those precious things your baby does.

Years from now, you'll be glad you did! (And so will your baby.)

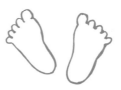

Expect to fall in love every day.

Be patient with yourself.
This is definitely
on-the-job training.

A New Mom Blessing

Heavenly Father,
Protect this beautiful mother
and her uniquely perfect
and precious child.
Give calm and assurance
to their journey.
Nourish them with
Your love and grace.

Go with the flow

will come to have many
new meanings.

Enjoy them all!

Whatever you
dream
for your baby,
be sure to keep dreaming
for yourself.

You will be richer for it.

Just think!

Your baby is going to learn how to love because of you.

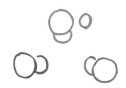

If cleanliness is next to Godliness,

a baby fresh from the bath is heaven on earth.

There is no
such thing as a
perfect mom!

Give yourself the same
compassion and understanding
you would give to others.

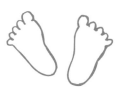

Record your **BABY's** laughter.

It's a sound worth saving forever.

Begin cultivating babysitters now.

At the first sign of cabin fever,

call one!

It's okay
to make time
for **yourself**.

*Your baby
needs the break too!*

You can never take too many pictures.

Make sure you are in some of them too!

Sweet Pea

Keep this little book
where you can see it often
so it will remind you
of the place
you hold in my heart.

And remember to stay healthy,
eat your peas!

photo
of
your sweet pea

Why Peas?

She was a vibrant, dazzling young woman with a promising future. Yet, at sixteen, her world felt sad and hopeless.

Though I was living over 1800 miles away, I wanted to let this very special young person in my life know that I would be there for her, across the miles and through the darkness. I wanted her to know she could call me any time, at any hour, and I would be there for her. And I wanted to give her a piece of my heart that she could take with her anywhere—a reminder that she was loved.

Really loved.

Her name is Maddy, and she was the inspiration for my first book in the Eat Your Peas series, *Eat Your Peas for Young Adults*. At the very beginning of her book, I made a place to write in my phone number so she would know I was serious about being available. And right beside the phone number, I put my promise to listen—truly listen—whenever that call came.

Soon after the book was published, people began to ask me if I had the same promise and affirmation for adults. It was then that I realized it isn't just young people who need to be reminded of how truly special they are. We all do.

Today, Maddy is thriving and giving hope to others in her life. I like to think that, in some way, I and my book were part of helping her achieve that. If someone has given you this book, it means *you are a pretty amazing person* to them, and they wanted to let you know. Take it to heart.

Believe it, and remind yourself often.

Wishing you peas and plenty of joy,

Cheryl Karpen

P.S. My mama always said, "Eat your peas! They're good for you." The pages of this book are filled with nutrients for your heart. They're simply good for you too.

About the author "Eat Your Peas"

A self-proclaimed dreamer, Cheryl
spends her time imagining and creating
between the historic river town of Anoka, Minnesota
and the seaside village of Islamorada, Florida.

An effervescent speaker, Cheryl brings inspiration,
insight, and humor to corporations,
professional organizations, and churches.
Learn more about her at www.cherylkarpen.com

If this book has touched your life,
Cheryl would like to hear your story.
Please send it to mystory@eatyourpeas.com.

About the illustrator

Sandy Fougner artfully weaves
a love for design, illustration and
interiors with being a wife
and mother of three sons.

The Eat Your Peas® Collection

now available:

Eat Your Peas® for Mom
Eat Your Peas® Daughter
Eat Your Peas® Faithfully, From Mom
Eat Your Peas® Faithfully
Eat Your Peas® Girlfriend

To Let You Know I Care
Hope for a Hurting Heart

Eat Your Peas® New Mom

Published in Nashville, Tennessee, by Thomas Nelson®.

Thomas Nelson is a trademark of Thomas Nelson, Inc.

Unless stated otherwise, Scripture quotations are from the *Holy Bible*, New Living Translation. © 1996. Used by permission of Tyndale House Publishers, Inc., Wheaton, Ill. 60189. All rights reserved.

Other quotations are taken from HOLY BIBLE: NEW INTERNATIONAL VERSION® (NIV). © 1973, 1978, 1984 by International Bible Society. Used by permission of Zondervan Publishing House. All rights reserved. THE NEW KING JAMES VERSION (NKJV). © 1982, 1992 by Thomas Nelson, Inc. Used by permission. All rights reserved.

Cover design by Koechel Peterson & Associates Minneapolis, MN

ISBN-13: 978-1-4041-9008-5

Printed in China

11 12 13 14 15 [RRD] 5 4 3 2 1

www.thomasnelson.com